the little book of
FRIENDSHIP

lucy lane

summersdale

THE LITTLE BOOK OF FRIENDSHIP

Summersdale Publishers Ltd
46 West Street
Chichester
West Sussex
PO19 1RP
UK

www.summersdale.com

Printed and bound in the Czech Republic

ISBN: 978-1-84953-862-6

Substantial discounts on bulk quantities of Summersdale books are available to corporations, professional associations and other organisations. For details contact Nicky Douglas by telephone: +44 (0) 1243 756902, fax: +44 (0) 1243 786300 or email: nicky@summersdale.com.

INTRODUCTION

Friendship is one of the true cornerstones of happiness. Even from an early age, we are inclined to form bonds with new people – to learn about them and learn from them. Some connections might last for moments, like a common courtesy paid to a stranger; some might last for years, in a lifelong relationship; but one thing is for certain: each of our friendships enriches us. This collection of inspiring suggestions and joyful quotations will remind you to cherish the friendships in your life – and always to be open to new ones.

FLEXIBLE FRIENDS

The beauty of friendships is that they exist in all shapes and sizes. You might consider one person alone to be your best friend, but that doesn't mean you can't have friendships with people in every sphere of your life, from the postman you sometimes chat to, to the work colleague you regularly confide in. Friendships can happen any 'where' and any 'when' – you never know how the next one will come about!

Friendship... that moment when one person says to another: 'You too? I thought I was the only one.'

C. S. Lewis

Love is being
stupid together.

Paul Valéry

SMILE, YOU'RE NOT ON CAMERA

A good friendship needs care and attention in order to flourish. It has become a social habit to document your time in photographs or on social media, which can be a distraction and hinder you from being a good participant and listener. Consider literally switching off when you spend time with friends, giving them your full attention.

True friendship comes when the silence between two people is comfortable.

David Tyson Gentry

There is nothing I would
not do for those who
are really my friends.

Jane Austen

ENJOY YOURSELVES

With lots of pressures in our lives, it is easy to fall into a pattern of using a friendship as a sounding board for our problems. If you feel a friendship has been all function and no fun, set aside a day where complaints and issues are banned. Discuss the good things in your lives or simply spend the day enjoying yourselves.

Laughter is the sound
of the soul dancing.

Jarod Kintz

'Tis the privilege of friendship to talk nonsense, and to have her nonsense respected.

Charles Lamb

GET OUT OF THE COMFORT ZONE

Like any relationship, a friendship needs to be maintained. Often, any time spent with a friend is a good time, but make sure you don't take each other for granted. Put the spark back into a friendship by trying something new together – sharing a new experience can bring you closer and show you new sides of your friend.

FRIENDS ARE PART OF THE GLUE THAT HOLDS LIFE AND FAITH TOGETHER.

Jon Katz

If you give people a
chance, they shine.

Billy Connolly

LET IT GO

All friends have their disagreements. If there is a problem that you and a friend are struggling to move on from and you feel you've tried your best to resolve it, ask yourself, 'Is this issue worth ending our friendship over?' We are all different, and having a differing opinion on a topic does not have to be a friendship-ending event. Consider agreeing to disagree for the sake of the friendship.

Some people go to priests, others to poetry, I to my friends.

Virginia Woolf

Whoever is happy will make others happy too.

Anne Frank

GO WILD

Both spending time in nature and spending time with friends can have a de-stressing effect on our mental health. Why not combine the two and go for a walk or visit a place of natural beauty with a friend? Not only will the fun you enjoy with your friend have a beautiful backdrop, but you'll feel better for it!

Mix a little foolishness with your **serious** plans. It is lovely to be **silly** at the right moment.

Horace

What is a friend?
I will tell you. It is a
person with whom you
dare to be yourself.

Frank Crane

SAY IT WITH... WORDS

Although you know in your heart how much you care for a friend, consider whether you've made them fully aware of your feelings. Although it can seem like you and your friend share the same brain, they're not actually a mind reader! Take a moment the next time you see your buddy to tell them how much they mean to you – it will make their day!

Each friend represents
a world in us, a world
possibly not born
until they arrive.

Anaïs Nin

Where there is love
there is life.

Mahatma Gandhi

OPPOSITES ATTRACT

Although you may think that you and your best pal are a bona fide odd couple, you're likely to find even stranger pairings in the animal kingdom. In Africa, Bubbles the elephant and Bella the Labrador are famous besties, and in the US, in a story straight out of a children's film, Baloo the bear, Shere Khan the tiger and Leo the lion, all fully grown real-life animals, are close friends!

CARRY LAUGHTER WITH YOU WHEREVER YOU GO.

Hugh Sidey

The friend who holds
your hand and says the
wrong thing is made
of dearer stuff than the
one who stays away.

Barbara Kingsolver

IT'S THE LITTLE THINGS

It can be easy to neglect the little pleasantries that can help enrich a friendship. Set aside some time each week to contact a friend you haven't talked to for a while. Ask them how they are and how their day was and remind them that you're thinking of them. You'll find it costs very little effort and reaps very big rewards.

A friend is one of the
nicest things you can
have, and one of the
best things you can be.

Douglas Pagels

He has achieved
success who has lived
well, laughed often,
and loved much.

Bessie Anderson Stanley

QUALITY NOT QUANTITY

Anthropologist Robert Dunbar has proposed that the number of relationships (of all kinds) a human can comfortably maintain is around 150. Don't worry about pressure from social media sites to have large amounts of 'friends' and 'followers'; it's perfectly natural to put your energy into maintaining your closest friendships rather than keeping up with that one person you met at a friend's party ten years ago!

I think that **beauty** comes from being **happy** and connected to the people we love.

Marcia Cross

A friend is someone
who knows all about
you and still loves you.

Elbert Hubbard

LOVE YOURSELF AS WELL AS OTHERS

Remember to extend the same kindnesses and courtesies that you offer your friends to yourself. Be forgiving about your faults, support yourself in your efforts to achieve and be mindful of your accomplishments. Not only is it beneficial to your own physical and mental health, but you can only be expected to support others if you're able to support yourself.

I would rather walk
with a friend in the dark,
than alone in the light.

Helen Keller

The Eskimo has fifty-two names for snow because it is important to them; there ought to be as many for love.

Margaret Atwood

ONE LOVE

A study at the University of Virginia found that friendships can help activate our ability to empathise. Researchers revealed that the subjects' brainwaves were the same when they were placed in danger as when their friend was placed in danger, showing evidence that we view a threat to our friends as a threat to ourselves. A good ability to empathise can help us become kinder and more understanding of others.

WHEREVER YOU GO, GO WITH ALL YOUR HEART.

Confucius

Silence makes the real conversations between friends. Not the saying, but the never needing to say that counts.

Margaret Lee Runbeck

A TREASURE CHEST

Collect photos and souvenirs of special moments that you've shared with a friend. This could be an excellent gift to share with a friend to show them how much they mean to you, or even a treat for yourself to act as a tribute to your relationship.

Friendship consists in forgetting what one gives and remembering what one receives.

Alexander Dumas

True happiness comes
from the joy of deeds
well done, the zest of
creating things new.

Antoine de Saint-Exupéry

CRAFT TOGETHER, LAUGH TOGETHER

Friendships can sometimes be expensive; lunches out, coffees, entry fees and presents can all add up. Sharing a craft hobby with a friend can be a great way to add some fun to the time you spend together without breaking the bank – you do something outside of the usual *and* you get to learn and create with your buddy.

It's the **friends** you can call up at 4 a.m. that **matter.**

Marlene Dietrich

Laughter is the
shortest distance
between two people.

Victor Borge

FRIENDS IN UNLIKELY PLACES

Studies have shown that having friends at your workplace can make you more creative, productive and even happier! Although you've been thrown together by circumstance, don't dismiss your colleagues as sources of companionship and support. Besides, you spend so much time together, you might as well get along!

One does not
make friends. One
recognises them.

Garth Henrichs

I'd far rather be happy
than right any day.

Douglas Adams

HAPPY BIRTHDAY TO US

A long-lasting friendship is an achievement, as well as a source of great happiness. Consider celebrating your relationship by holding a 'birthday' party for a long-lived friendship; invite your buddy over for an indulgent night in or get out to your favourite pub, bar or restaurant. It will reinforce the good elements of your relationship and provide an opportunity for some silliness and much reminiscing.

OUR SOULMATE IS THE ONE WHO MAKES LIFE COME TO LIFE.

Richard Bach

Wherever we are, it
is our friends that
make our world.

Henry Drummond

LISTEN UP

When talking with a friend, remember to really listen to what they are saying. Don't assume that you already know everything they think or have to say; put aside distractions when conversing and really consider their words. It may be they have changed in a way that you haven't noticed or they need your support at the moment. Even if that isn't the case, it's always nice to feel that you have someone's full attention.

A snowball in the face is surely the perfect beginning to a lasting friendship.

Markus Zusak

Laugh and the world
laughs with you.

Ella Wheeler Wilcox

ALL THINGS BEING EQUAL

Humans can have a strong sense of fairness and are often keenly aware when a relationship appears unequal or that one party is giving more. However, if you are feeling resentful of a friend for this reason, take a moment to check on your circumstances. Every friendship has its ebbs and flows; it may be that a friend is in need of some support and doesn't have the resources to be there for you as they'd like. Have patience and your generosity will soon be reciprocated.

Life is a helluva lot
more **fun** if you say
'yes' rather than 'no'.

Richard Branson

The finest kind of
friendship is between
people who expect
a great deal of each
other but never ask it.

Sylvia Bremer

HAVE A REST(IE)
WITH THE BESTIE

We can't be busy all the time or else we'd collapse. Even if you're the sort of person to flourish when your life is all go, reward yourself with a little downtime to refresh your mind and your body. But relaxing doesn't have to be a one-person activity – invite a friend round to veg on the sofa with a cup of something hot and a little background noise.

In prosperity our friends
know us; in adversity
we know our friends.

John Churton Collins

In dreams and in
love there are no
impossibilities.

János Arany

SHARE YOUR LOVE

A good thing can be made brilliant when it is shared with friends. If you've read a corker of a book or seen a blindingly good film on DVD, lend it to your friends. It can spark interesting and rich conversation as you discuss your points of view, whether you both loved it or not! Similarly, if a friend offers to lend you something they loved, take the chance, even if it doesn't sound up your street. You might be surprised!

YOU NEVER LOSE
BY LOVING.

Barbara De Angelis

Friendship is a
sheltering tree.

Samuel Taylor Coleridge

Everything in our life
should be based on love.

Ray Bradbury

NIGGLES

Nobody is perfect – not even you! While good communication and honest feedback is an important element of relationship maintenance, so is the ability to separate the big issues from the little niggles. For example, while it might bear serious discussion if someone is constantly hours late to your appointments, weigh up the effect a few minutes' tardiness has on your daily life and whether it seriously upsets you or only costs you a little annoyance.

Friends are the
family you choose.

Jess C. Scott

What the world really
needs is more love
and less paperwork.

Pearl Bailey

TASTES LIKE FRIENDSHIP

Next time you're having a get-together, ask everyone to bring a dish they've made themselves (or bought, if the kitchen is not their arena). Your table will be a visual model of your friendship, with each dish representing the good things your friend brings to your life – and you'll get to enjoy a feast, too!

'Stay' is a charming
word in a friend's
vocabulary.

Amos Bronson Alcott

The best thing to hold
on to in life is each other.

Audrey Hepburn

SAY IT OUT LOUD

Support your friends as you would like to be supported. We are all fellow humans, trying our best in sometimes challenging circumstances. Speak up when a friend has done something they are proud of, or even something you think they should be proud of, and congratulate them on their achievements. You will make your friend feel great and you get to share their special moment.

INTO THE HOUSE WHERE JOY LIVES, HAPPINESS WILL GLADLY COME.

Japanese proverb

A friend is somebody
you want to be around
when you feel like
being by yourself.

Barbara Burrow

NOT EVEN ONCE

Trust is a special part of our bond with friends. But it can be fragile, and broken trust can seriously harm a good friendship. If a friend has shared a secret with you, don't pass it on to others, even if you think there's no harm in it. It is entirely up to your friend what they choose to share of their life and with whom.

The love we give away is
the only love we keep.

Elbert Hubbard

It is not so much our friends' help that helps us, as the confidence of their help.

Epicurus

SHAKE, RATTLE AND ROLL

Exercise is a necessary (and often challenging) part of life, and unless your particular pleasure is donning Lycra and dashing about the place, finding the motivation to do all we should can be hard. Pairing up with an exercise buddy can be a great way to provide and receive support; what is painful on your own can often be hilarious with a companion.

There is **nothing** on this earth more to be prized than true **friendship**.

St Thomas Aquinas

Nothing shows a man's character more than what he laughs at.

Johann Wolfgang von Goethe

A SUPERSTAR FOR A DAY

Hire a room in a karaoke bar with friends and have an evening of complete, unabashed silliness singing along to golden oldies, cheesy ballads and epic rock hits. It is wonderfully freeing to let your inner child out with people you trust. Alternative suggestions for the musically impaired: go skinny-dipping, put on a play or make a big sandcastle at the beach.

A good laugh is
sunshine in a house.

William Makepeace Thackeray

Friendship is the only cement that will ever hold the world together.

Woodrow Wilson

THE HARDEST WORD

Even if you are having a problem with a friend, remember that you are a team. You should be working together to find a solution rather than against each other in order to 'win'. Realise that even if it wasn't your intention, your action may have hurt your friend, and be generous with your apologies. The word 'sorry', genuinely meant, can be a soothing balm to sore feelings.

FRIENDSHIP
IMPROVES
HAPPINESS, AND
ABATES MISERY,
BY DOUBLING
OUR JOYS
AND DIVIDING
OUR GRIEF.

Marcus Tullius Cicero

Always be a first-rate version of yourself, instead of a second-rate version of somebody else.

Judy Garland

BEST FRIENDS FOREVER

Scientists at the University of Chicago have discovered that babies as young as nine months old are aware of the concept of friendship. It seems that, with humans being social animals, friendship comes naturally to us. How lovely!

Friendship... has no survival value; rather it is one of those things which give value to survival.

C. S. Lewis

The language of
friendship is not
words but meanings.

Henry David Thoreau

PAYBACK TIME

Remember the times when friends came through for you in a big way and look for opportunities to repay them down the line. For example, offering a crate of wine is a great thank you for that time they helped you move, but the gift of your time freely given when a friend is in need will be even more precious. (But don't hold back on the wine.)

Wishing to be friends is quick work, but **friendship** is a slow ripening fruit.

Aristotle

There are no traffic jams
along the extra mile.

Roger Staubach

FREE AND EASY

If you are looking for a fun, free day out with friends, check out what's happening in your local community. Summertime is a particularly busy season with community fairs, food festivals and local outdoor events, but winter can also feature indoor craft fairs, concerts and winter markets. Not only are these events a great way to spend the day with a friend but they also help your involvement in your community.

Have a heart that never
hardens, and a temper
that never tires, and a
touch that never hurts.

Charles Dickens

There is nothing better than a friend, unless it is a friend with chocolate.

Linda Grayson

COW DO YOU DO?

Cows reportedly have best friends; not only do the farmyard animals prefer hanging out in groups and experience stress when isolated, but they have particular companions that they prefer spending time with. Cows – they're just like us!

LAUGHTER TO ME IS BEING ALIVE.

William Saroyan

The most beautiful
discovery true friends
make is that they
can grow separately
without growing apart.

Elizabeth Foley

JOIN THE CLUB

Our friends often become our friends because we share similar interests or opinions. Get back to the roots of your friendship by joining a local organisation or even starting one yourselves, depending on your hobby. You'll get to meet even more like-minded people and spend your leisure time doing the things you love with the people you love.

Tell me who admires
and loves you and I will
tell you who you are.

Charles-Augustin Sainte-Beuve

A friend knows the song in my heart and sings it to me when my memory fails.

Donna Roberts

DON'T BE AFRAID OF QUIET TIMES

It is said that the mark of a good friendship is one that lasts through periods of quiet and non-contact. Anybody can have the feeling of 'life getting in the way'. As long as you let friends know that you're busy, there's no harm in being socially unavailable for a little while. You'll see each other soon and catch up on everything you've missed!

If you have **two** friends in your lifetime, you're **lucky**. If you have one good friend, you're **more** than lucky.

S. E. Hinton

Wrinkles should merely
indicate where the
smiles have been.

Mark Twain

IN A LIFETIME

It is estimated that a single person goes through around 396 friendships of varying levels of attachment in their lifetime, although only a handful of these will be considered 'close' friends. It seems that although we have more social opportunities in the modern age, we really do treasure having a few special friends.

We build too many walls
and not enough bridges.

Isaac Newton

Let us be grateful to people who make us happy; they are the charming gardeners who make our souls blossom.

Marcel Proust

FAMILY VALUES

Friends are the family we choose. Be upfront about appreciating the support and love given to you by your friend-family and reciprocate wherever you can. Show a friend just how much they mean to you by writing them a heartfelt thank-you card – it doesn't need to be a special occasion to let them know that you care.

WORDS ARE EASY, LIKE THE WIND; FAITHFUL FRIENDS ARE HARD TO FIND.

William Shakespeare

Try to be like the turtle –
at ease in your own shell.

Bill Copeland

GET COMPETITIVE

Whether your arena is the outdoors, the games console or a board game, a little healthy competition can be good for friendships. Host an event for a group of your friends with snacks and small prizes for the winners (and losers). You'll get the adrenaline racing and the banter flowing.

Always do what is right. It will gratify half of mankind and astound the other.

Mark Twain

Be slow to fall into
friendship; but when
thou art in, continue
firm and constant.

Socrates

Always laugh
when you can. It is
cheap medicine.

Lord Byron

CHOP CHOP

Try signing up to a cooking class or wine-tasting course together. Learning with friends is twice the fun! And you'll gain impressive new skills that you can share with others – consider inviting a group of friends around for a home-cooked meal or a BBQ to show off your new culinary flair – you might even be able to gain extra points by matching the food perfectly with the wine you serve.

Leave something for someone but don't leave someone for something.

Enid Blyton

FRIENDSHIP IS LIKE MONEY, EASIER MADE THAN KEPT.

Samuel Butler

Give out what you most
want to come back.

Robin Sharma

THE BAD WITH THE GOOD

A Canadian study discovered that it was just as important for friends to know each other's dislikes as their likes. It seems obvious but the relationships where friends were conscious of each other's irritants were stronger and had less conflict than those where friends were unaware – the buddies knew to avoid the behaviours and topics most likely to set off their friend.

We often take for
granted the very things
that most deserve
our gratitude.

Cynthia Ozick

Love is blind; friendship closes its eyes.

Anonymous

MAKE MEMORIES

Don't be afraid to splash some cash on the friendship. While being frugal is a good long-term plan, adventures are an important part of life, and who better to enjoy them with than your best friends? Plan a trip to a dream destination or a luxury event and do something that you will remember for the rest of your life.

Friendship isn't a big thing. It's a **million** little things.

Anonymous

Shared joy is a double
joy; shared sorrow
is half a sorrow.

Swedish proverb

BE YOURSELF

When you are doubting yourself, remember, your friends love you for who you are. Your quirks are what make you special and what speak to their own little oddities. If you are really struggling, ask your friends what they like about you. They'll soon give you a boost in confidence.

I can trust my friends.
These people force me
to examine myself,
encourage me to grow.

Cher

However rare true love
may be, it is less so
than true friendship.

Albert Einstein

DON'T HOLD BACK

We often see things that remind us of our friends. If you spot a little something you think they'll love, don't wait around for an occasion: snap it up now and give them an impromptu gift. It will make their day to know you were thinking of them.

A FAITHFUL FRIEND IS THE MEDICINE OF LIFE.

Ben Sira

Whatever you are,
be a good one.

Abraham Lincoln

PEN PALS

There are many advantages to quick-fire communication, but it can lack the thoughtfulness and sense of 'special occasion' that a handwritten letter can have. Write a missive to a friend, whether you live next door or hundreds of miles away! You might find it's easier to say things this way, and your friend will also have a lovely keepsake of your relationship.

Who, being loved,
is poor?

Oscar Wilde

I don't need a friend
who changes when I
change and who nods
when I nod; my shadow
does that much better.

Plutarch

LOVE AND FRIENDSHIP

Anthropologist Robin Dunbar has discovered that when a new love enters your life they usually displace one or two friends. We all deserve to enjoy friends *and* a beloved, but if you've been swept up in the throes of love, consider doing a little friend maintenance. Check in with your pals and arrange to meet or talk; you might be surprised that it's been longer than you thought.

True friendship is like
sound **health**; the
value of it is seldom
known until it be **lost**.

Charles Caleb Colton

Being deeply loved
by someone gives
you strength, while
loving someone deeply
gives you courage.

Lao Tzu

HONESTY IS MOSTLY THE BEST POLICY

You should always be able to be honest and truthful with friends. However, to quote Mary Ann Pietzker, 'Is it true? Is it necessary? Is it kind?' If you have something difficult to say to a friend, ensure that the answer to these three questions is 'yes' before speaking. This will cut any nit-picking or accidental cruelty from your statement.

Sometimes the
heart sees what is
invisible to the eye.

H. Jackson Brown Jr

Friendship – my definition – is built on two things. Respect and trust.

Stieg Larsson

BE INCLUSIVE

One of the best things in life is to have fun with friends. Be aware, though, that we all have different means and abilities. If you love running but your friend isn't as able, or fine dining is your thing but it's out of your friend's budget, find things to do that you're able to participate in equally. You may not end up doing as much of your favourite activity but you will spend more time with your favourite person.

TRUE FRIENDSHIP
ISN'T ABOUT
BEING THERE
WHEN IT'S
CONVENIENT.
IT'S ABOUT
BEING THERE
WHEN IT'S NOT.

Anonymous

A journey is best
measured in friends
rather than miles.

Tim Cahill

TIME TRAVEL

Although one shouldn't always be living in the past, don't be afraid to wallow in some fantastic memories with friends. Host a theme night reminiscent of a great time you shared, perhaps a holiday or a fab day trip. Recreate the food and drink you had, haul out the photos and videos and split your sides laughing about the good time you shared.

Don't walk in front of me; I may not follow. Just walk beside me and be my friend.

Albert Camus

I always felt that the great high privilege, relief and comfort of friendship, was that one had to explain nothing.

Katherine Mansfield

FEELING GOOD

Friends offer us more than just support and a good time. Studies show that people with a large circle of friends suffer less stress, are less depressed and even have a stronger immune system. It seems that friends encourage us into healthy habits (except maybe that one friend who always encourages you to have another slice of cake).

Those who bring **sunshine** into the lives of others cannot keep it from **themselves.**

J. M. Barrie

One cannot have
too large a party.

Jane Austen

BUY THE TICKET

If you remember having your parents attend the school play you were acting in, or your concert or recital, you'll recall how good it felt to have them there watching your endeavours. Although as adults our hobbies are often private affairs, if a friend is performing or attending a craft fair or entering a race, turn up and support them! It means the world to have a friendly face in the audience when you're trying your hardest.

Love all, trust a few,
do wrong to none.

William Shakespeare

The most wasted of all
days is that in which
we have not laughed.

Nicolas Chamfort

A PROBLEM SHARED

Feeling ill is rough on most people, even when you only have a cold. If a friend is poorly, check in with them to see how they're holding up. While you don't have to blow their nose, a little sympathy and some homemade food goes a long way to making a person feel cared for.

WHEN WE GIVE CHEERFULLY AND ACCEPT GRATEFULLY, EVERYONE IS BLESSED.

Maya Angelou

One joy scatters a
hundred griefs.

Chinese proverb

CELEBRATE GOOD TIMES

The most important part of friendship is that you enjoy each other's company and improve each other's lives. It's healthy to ask yourself from time to time whether you're being a good friend but as long as you're sharing good times, that's all that matters!

There are two ways of spreading light: to be the candle or the mirror that reflects it.

Edith Wharton

A good **companion** shortens the **longest** road.

Turkish proverb

My best friend is the
one who brings out
the best in me.

Henry Ford

the little book of
RESILIENCE

lucy lane

ISBN: 978-1-84953-830-5

the little book of
RELAXATION

lucy lane

ISBN: 978-1-84953-787-2

the little book of
POSITIVITY

lucy lane

ISBN: 978-1-84953-788-9

the little book of
MEDITATIONS

gilly pickup

ISBN: 978-1-84953-864-0

the little book of
AFFIRMATIONS

gilly pickup

ISBN: 978-1-84953-863-3

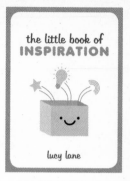

the little book of
INSPIRATION

lucy lane

ISBN: 978-1-84953-843-5

the little book of
COMFORT

lucy lane

ISBN: 978-1-84953-793-3

the little book of
HAPPINESS

lucy lane

ISBN: 978-1-84953-790-2

If you're interested in finding out
more about our books, find us on
Facebook at **Summersdale Publishers**
and follow us on Twitter
at **@Summersdale**.

www.summersdale.com